CRITICALLY ACCLAIMED!

Hear is the book that thowzands of those of Polish extrakshun (and prowd of it!) have been waiting for! I red every joke and almost split my sides laffing. I sent one to my mother for Mother's Day and all she did waz beg for three dozinn more. And my girlfriend (who's half Polish, half crazy), all she wants to do theze days is reed this book—I always knew she could never get enuff, but this is ridikulus! I hope that all those other ethnik groops will buy it too. Then they will no that Poles aint as dumb as they think.

—Stanislas Paznanski; Literary Editor
The Hamtrack Polish-American Bugle

Also by Larry Wilde from Pinnacle Books

THE OFFICIAL BEDROOM/BATHROOM JOKE BOOK
MORE THE OFFICIAL SMART KIDS/DUMB PARENTS
    JOKE BOOK
THE OFFICIAL BOOK OF SICK JOKES
MORE THE OFFICIAL JEWISH/IRISH JOKE BOOK
THE LAST OFFICIAL ITALIAN JOKE BOOK
THE OFFICIAL CAT LOVERS/DOG LOVERS JOKE BOOK
THE OFFICIAL DIRTY JOKE BOOK
THE LAST OFFICIAL POLISH JOKE BOOK
THE OFFICIAL GOLFERS JOKE BOOK
THE OFFICIAL SMART KIDS/DUMB PARENTS JOKE BOOK
THE OFFICIAL RELIGIOUS/NOT SO RELIGIOUS JOKE BOOK
MORE THE OFFICIAL POLISH/ITALIAN JOKE BOOK
THE OFFICIAL BLACK FOLK/WHITE FOLKS JOKE BOOK
THE OFFICIAL VIRGINS/SEX MANIACS JOKE BOOK
THE OFFICIAL JEWISH/IRISH JOKE BOOK
THE OFFICIAL POLISH/ITALIAN JOKE BOOK
THE COMPLETE BOOK OF ETHNIC HUMOR
THE OFFICIAL POLISH JOKE BOOK
THE OFFICIAL ITALIAN JOKE BOOK
THE OFFICIAL CAT LOVERS JOKE BOOK
THE OFFICIAL WILDE AND DIRTY JOKE BOOK

THE OFFICIAL
POLISH JOKE BOOK

Larry Wilde

PINNACLE BOOKS NEW YORK

THE OFFICIAL POLISH JOKE BOOK

Copyright © 1973, 1981 by Larry Wilde

Illustrations copyright © 1973, 1981 by Pinnacle Books, Inc.

An original Pinnacle Books edition.

First printing/April 1981
Thirtieth printing/September 1985

ISBN: 0-523-42606-2
Can. ISBN: 0-523-43553-3

Printed in the United States of America

PINNACLE BOOKS, INC.
1430 Broadway
New York, New York 10018

With special thanks to Professor Dan Desmond for his invaluable assistance.

CONTENTS

INTRODUCTION

The book you are holding is somewhat unique. It is the largest selling (over one million copies) collection of jokes in the history of publishing.

Never before has a gag fad lasted as long or been as popular as the Polish joke. It is truly a phenomenon in humor circles.

Ethnic jokes have been around since Biblical times. Humor historians claim that man has always poked fun at some race or religious group. It just happens that today, these barbed jests are directed toward Americans of Polish descent.

Through the years, in the United States, other victims have been Jews, blacks, Germans, Mexicans, Puerto Ricans, Italians, and the Irish. Not to overlook the Swedes living in and around Minneapolis, Finns, near Fitchburg, Massachusetts, and the original Americans, the foot, pony, and cliff Indians.

In the 1880s newly arrived Sons of Erin were referred to as "micks" and "greenhorns" and were lampooned for their speech, manners, and alleged ignorance.

The following gag is typical of what convulsed the boys down at the corner saloon:

Mrs. Murphy and Mrs. O'Connor were on their way back from church. "Me son, Jimmy's comin' home tomorra!" said Mrs. Murphy.

"That's nice!" replied Mrs. O'Connor. "But I thought he was sent up fer five years."

"That's true!" answered her companion. "But he got time off fer good behavior!"

"Oh, my," said her friend. "It must be a blessin' to you, to know you've got such a fine son!"

During the influx of Spanish-speaking peoples from San Juan, the popular put-down around New York had as its tag a line from a well-known song.

What is the Puerto Rican National Anthem? (singing) We'll take Manhattan, the Bronx and Staten Island, too!

Probably the longest continuous tirade of mockery (*a couple of thousand years*) has been aimed at those of the Jewish faith. Witness this one typical example of anti-Semitic derision:

How did the Grand Canyon come about? A Jew dropped a penny down a gopher hole.

If that below-the-belt jab wasn't painful enough, here's a little solar-plexis punch from out of the dark prejudiced past:

Why do Jews have large noses?
Because the air is free.

Dating back to the days of vaudeville, Polish-Americans around Buffalo, Detroit, and Milwaukee suffered humiliating cracks about themselves (little knowing that one day Polish jokes would become a national craze).

The wisecrack is a traditional form of the American jest. The core of its effectiveness comes from somebody being the butt of the joke, for it is always easier to laugh when someone else is being ridiculed.

And yet isn't that the greatness of America? That we live in a land where telling any kind of joke is permitted? That our right of free speech enables us to poke fun at even the most sacred elements of our social and cultural value system?

Psychiatrists contend that the higher the intelligence the greater the sense of humor. And therein lies the key. The ability to laugh at oneself.

Of course, when one is a member of a minority and the object of the barb, one must have a super king-sized funny bone. He just has to accept the fact that it is a gag. It's all in fun.

On the following pages you will find the best—or the worst, depending on your sensibilities and sense of humor—of the Polish jokes currently making the rounds.

As the fellow once said, "Laugh, and the world laughs with you."

Larry Wilde

THE OFFICIAL POLISH JOKEBOOK

GOLABKI

How do you get a Polack up on the roof?
Tell him the beer is on the house.

* * *

Why can't Polish farmers grow rabbits?
Because they plant them too deep.

* * *

Krupsak complained to his neighbor, Dobrienski that his house was being overrun with rats.

"Here's what you do," said Dobrienski. "Just pour boiling water into their holes."

Three days later they met again. "That be good idea of yours but it no work," said Krupsak. "I can't find nobody to hold the rats."

* * *

News Flash
Polish scientists announced today that they have just come up with the first test-tube miscarriage.

Jensen finished his dinner in a small Detroit diner and asked Alina, the waitress, "What flavors of ice cream do you have?"

She answered in a hoarse whisper, "Vanilla, strawberry, and chocolate."

"You got laryngitis?" asked Jensen, sympathetically.

"No," said the Polish waitress, "just vanilla, strawberry, and chocolate."

* * *

Polish Girl: Mama, I'm pregnant.
Mother: Are you sure it's yours?

* * *

How can you tell where a Polack lives?
He's the only one in the neighborhood who has crabgrass inside the house.

Szymczyk went to the pet shop to complain about his canary that wouldn't sing. The owner said, "File the beak just a little bit, and the bird will sing. But if you file it too much the canary will die."

Two weeks later the owner ran into Szymczyk on the street and inquired about his canary. "He died," said the Pole.

"But I told you not to file the beak too much."

"I didn't," said the Polack, "but by the time I got him out of the vise he be already dead."

* * *

Zientek was on an elevator with several other passengers. As the elevator moved up, he stared at the small fan slowly turning in the elevator ceiling. "It be amazing," said the Polack to the other people, "that such a small fan can lift all these people."

"Someone just stole my car," shouted Sullivan after leaving his keys in his car.

"Don't worry," said Stadnicki, "I got the license number!"

* * *

Piotr introduced himself to a cute chick in a cocktail lounge. After a while he asked her for a date. "I never date Polacks," she told him.

"How you know I Polack," asked Piotr.

"You have B.O. and you're wearing your boots on the wrong feet," she replied.

* * *

In the Olympics, the Polish javelin team lost. They won the toss and elected to receive.

* * *

A customer said to the Polish waitress, "Do you know whether the milk from this dairy is pasteurized?"

"It sure is," answered the girl, "Every morning they turn their cows out to pasture."

A survey was being taken on a Michigan college campus. The survey taker asked a Polish football player, "What do you think of bilingualism?"

"I think it's okay," said the Polack, "if it's between two consenting adults."

* * *

Gabreski came home and found his house on fire. He rushed next door, telephoned the fire department, and shouted, "Hurry over here. My house be on fire."

"Okay," replied the fireman. "How do we get there?"

"Say," yelled the Polack, "don't you still have those big red trucks?"

* * *

The Polish Government has just announced their solution to the oil shortage:

Import 200 tons of Arabian sand and drill our own wells.

UNIVERSITY OF WARSAW
ENTRANCE EXAM *

1 SAND	2 MAN / BOARD	3 STAND / I	4 R|E|A|D|I|N|G
5 WEAR / UNDER	6 R ROADS D S	7 T O W N	8 CYCLE CYCLE CYCLE
9 LE VEL	10 O M.D. PH.D. B.S.	11 KNEE LIGHTS	12 II IIII ●●
13 CHAIR	14 DICE DICE	15 T O U C H	16 GROUND FEET FEET FEET FEET FEET FEET
17 MIND / MATTER	18 HE'S/HIMSELF	19 ECNALG	20 DEATH/LIFE

*Answers on page 8

Answers to University
of Warsaw Entrance Exam

1. Sandbox
2. Man overboard
3. I understand
4. Reading between the lines
5. Long underwear
6. Cross roads
7. Downtown
8. Tricycle
9. Splitlevel
10. Three degrees below zero
11. Neon lights
12. Circles under the eyes
13. Highchair
14. Paradise
15. Touchdown
16. Six feet underground
17. Mind over matter
18. He's by himself
19. A backward glance
20. Life after death

Four Polacks were driving in a pickup truck. Two were sitting up front in the cab. The other two were riding in the back.

The truck swerved around a sharp curve, crashed through a barrier, and wound up in a river. The truck sank immediately. The two Polacks up in the cab escaped and swam to shore. But the two Polacks riding in the back drowned.

They couldn't get the tailgate down!

*　*　*

Pieracki was mowing the lawn in his backyard when the lawn mower got away from him, crashed through his fence, and landed in his neighbor's swimming pool.

Lopez, the neighbor understood the situation. "Don't worry, amigo," said the Mexican, "I get it up for you."

He went in the house and came back with a mask, flippers, an entire scuba diving outfit. Lopez dove in the water, swam to the bottom of the pool, and took hold of the rope on the lawn mower motor. He began pulling on it unsuccessfully in hopes of starting it.

"You dumb beaner!" shouted Pieracki from the edge of the pool. "Choke it! Choke it!"

9

Polish tape: it's the same as Scotch tape except that it has no sticky side.

* * *

A Polack and a Mexican got married. Nine months later they had a baby. They named it Retardo!

* * *

Wojciechowicz applied for a job in a factory. The company doctor was giving him a physical examination. "Have your eyes ever been checked?" asked the M.D.

"No," answered the Polack. "They always be brown."

* * *

Modjeska and Kulez had been duck hunting since four o'clock in the morning and had only one duck. "We sure are lousy duck hunters," said Modjeska. "Let's go home."

"Nah!" appealed Kulez. "Let's stay longer."

"Something must be wrong," said Modjeska. "You think we not throwing the dogs up high enough?"

* * *

Bateman: Why don't you get an encyclopedia?
Wieslaw: It be too much work pumping up hills.

* * *

When did they realize the new pope was Polish?

When they saw he was wearing red sneakers.

* * *

Why have all dogs been banned from the Vatican?

Because they pee on Poles.

11

The pope's next pronouncement on birth control is to be titled:

Paul's Epistle to the Fallopians

* * *

Besides having a great sense of humor the new pope is a very neat man and has some fine decorating ideas. One of the things he wants to do is wallpaper the Sistine Chapel.

* * *

New Polish Prayer
Hail Mary, full of Grace
Now the Italians are in 2nd place

* * *

"You know how you're always rating girls on a scale of 1 to 10?"

"Yeah?"

"Well, what is a Polish 10?"

"I dunno."

"Five 2s!"

Why can't Poland field an ice hockey team?
Everybody drowns in spring training!

* * *

Personnel officer: What would you do if you
broke your arm in two places?
Kusielewicz: I wouldn't go to those places no
more.

* * *

ABC has announced that a Polish version of
"Roots" is being planned. It will be entitled,
"Weeds."

* * *

Newest drink in Poland:
Perrier water and club soda

An American, an Italian, and a Polack were captured by the Iranians and were sentenced to die for spying. "Listen," said the American to his friends, "The Iranians can be scared by the least little thing. Just before they're ready to shoot, yell something!"

They stood the American up against a wall. The Iranian sergeant shouted: "Ready! Aim! . . ." At that moment the American yelled, "Earthquake!" The Iranians scattered quickly and the American escaped.

They lined the Italian up at the wall. The sergeant ordered, "Ready! Aim! . . ." The Italian screamed, "Tornado!" The Iranians scampered away and the Italian escaped.

Twenty minutes later, the Iranians reorganized and put the Polack up against the wall. Again the NCO in charge ordered, "Ready! Aim! . . ."

And the Polack shouted, "Fire!"

"Hey, Joe, why you look so happy?"

"I just find out I can play my AM radio in the afternoon."

* * *

Then there was the Polack who bought two CBs so he could talk to himself.

* * *

News Item

The Poles have just ordered 2,000 septic tanks from the U.S. As soon as they learn to drive them, they are going to invade Germany.

* * *

Stash and Helen agreed to go to a new sexual encounter group in order to improve their physical relationship.

Two weeks later they were sitting in the living room and Stash said, "Sweetheart, I'd like to eat you down below."

"Oh, the school really helped. I'm glad you were honest."

"I always wanted to do it but it smells too bad. Why don't you go to the drugstore and get some of that hygiene stuff."

"Okay."

She returned an hour later all excited. "Oh, Stash," she exclaimed, "they have all kinds of flavors. Cherry, raspberry, strawberry . . ."

"Good. What kind you get?"

"Tuna!" said the Polish woman.

* * *

Lagoon:
French Polack

* * *

How can you tell a Polish airplane in a snowstorm?

It's the one with the chains on the propellers!

17

Costa, Gandolpho, and Domanski were about to visit the Godfather. "Remember now," warned Costa, "his grandson was born without ears, make sure you don't mention nothin' about the kid not havin' any ears!"

The three men entered the Godfather's living room where the Mafia chieftan was rocking his new grandson on his lap.

"Oh, Godfather," exclaimed Costa, "what beautiful hair the child has. He's gonna be a movie star."

"Thank you so much," replied the Godfather.

Gondolpho stepped forward and said, "What a big chest he's got, he's gonna be a football player!"

"Thanks a lot," said the elderly mobster.

"Say," said Domanski, "how's his eyes?"

"Oh, they're 20/20," answered the Godfather proudly.

"That's good," said the Polack, "cause the kid's never gonna wear glasses."

* * *

PIROGI

What's green, purple, orange, chartreuse, pink, and red?
A Polish housewife going to church on Sunday.

* * *

How many Polacks does it take to paint a house?
1,001.
One to hold the brush and 1,000 to move the house up and down.

* * *

What happened to the Polish National Library?
Somebody stole the book.

* * *

Polack Being Interviewed for a Job:
Interviewer: Your name is Bob?
Polack: Yes.
Interviewer: Do you spell it with two o's?

Why don't they have any ice cubes in Poland?
The inventor died and took the recipe with
him.

* * *

What is the smallest building in Poland?
The Polish Hall of Fame.

* * *

Brudzewa and Wlassak bought a Country
Squire station wagon with wooden sides. When
they got it home, they ripped off all the wood
paneling. When they'd finished, Brudzewa
said, "You know, I like wagon better when it
was in box!"

* * *

How do Polish dogs get snubbed noses?
From chasing parked cars.

What do the numbers 1776 and 1492 have in common?
They are adjoining rooms at the Warsaw Hilton.

* * *

Barry Glazer, Exec Producer and Director of Dick Clark's "American Bandstand" TV show, swears this happened at a taping:

"Harry, I got a great new Polish joke for you," said a cameraman to the floor manager.

"Okay, but just be careful," warned Harry. "Remember, I'm Polish!"

"All right," replied the cameraman, "I'll tell it to you very slowly."

* * *

Polish Ponderosa: Kosiuosko Park.

Comedian-dialectician Jeremy Vernon repeated this classic to me backstage at the Century Plaza Hotel: Kowalski and Resnicki were digging a cesspool. "How come we down here and Irish guy is upstairs in clear air?" said Kowalski. "All he got do is pull up bucket."

"By Joe, you right!" agreed Resnicki. "I go up and find out!"

"It'd be easier for me," said the Irishman, "to illustrate than to explain the reason." *He placed his hand flat against the wall and said:* "Hit my hand as hard as you can." Resnicki did. At the last second the Irishman yanked his hand away and Resnicki smashed his fist into the brick wall.

Down in the cesspool again, he said, "Kowalski, you want know why Irish guy is up there and we down here?"

"Yes!" said Kowalski.

"It be easier for me to illustrate than to explain reason." *Resnicki held his hand in front of his face and said:* "Hit my hand with shovel, hard as you can!"

* * *

Why does it take five men to give a Polack a shower?
One to hold him and four to spit.

25

Comic Lou Alexander tells about Kuchinski walking into the doctor's office with a frog on his head. "What seems to be the problem?" asked the physician.

And the frog said, "Well, it's about this wart on my behind."

* * *

Janicki and Bolewicz were strolling along the beach. Suddenly a sea gull flying overhead dropped a load. It hit Janicki right in the eye.

"I'll go get some toilet paper," offered Bolewicz.

"Don't bother," said Janicki. "He's probably miles away by now!"

* * *

Morris Diamond, Beverly Hills Records prez and cocktail party raconteur, tells about the man sitting next to a Polish woman on an airplane. She was carrying a baby in her arms.

The man said to her, "Lady, that is the ugliest baby I've ever seen! It looks like a monkey!"

The incensed woman called over the stewardess and said, "This man just insulted me! He called my baby a monkey!"

"Don't be upset," soothed the hostess. "I'll get you a drink and then I'll bring your lunch . . . and here's a banana for your baby!"

* * *

What do they call a dance attended by a bunch of Polacks?
A goof ball.

* * *

Why wasn't Christ born in Poland?
They couldn't find three wise men and a virgin.

27

Ned Sukin, New Jersey's top liquor sales-man, tells buyers about the Chicagoan who goes to the doctor for a brain transplant. "If you'd like to have a Jewish brain, it'll cost $10,000!" explained the M.D. "If you want a Polish brain, you'll have to pay $100,000!"

"I can understand the Jewish brain costing ten grand," said the Windy City resident, "Those people are pretty smart. But why is the other one so expensive?"

"Ah, Hah!" said the physician, "The Polish brain has never been used!"

* * *

What do they call a hoola hoop?
A teething ring for big-mouthed Polacks.

* * *

What is a Polish queer?
A guy who would rather go out with girls than go pick mushrooms.

Actress-interior decorator Cara Williams saves this one for special new friends: Poles up in arms over the slanderous remarks about their intelligence finally forced NASA to employ a Polish astronaut. On his first mission he was sent into space with just a monkey and told to watch the red light on his panel. When it lit up, he was to follow the prerecorded instructions. The green light provided commands for the monkey.

An hour after liftoff, the green light flashed and instructed the monkey: "You are now at stage one. Record speed. Regulate radiograph. Release retroactive regenerators!" And he did.

In a little while the green light lit up again and the monkey followed his orders: "Fire rockets. Adjust oxygen supply. Take temperature, blood pressure, and check pulse rate."

Four hours later, the red light came on and the Polish astronaut breathlessly awaited his first command. Over the loudspeaker came these instructions: "Feed the monkey!"

* * *

Polish National Bank: Pole Vault.

How do you make Polish Shishkabob?
You shoot a flaming arrow into a garbage can.

* * *

Why does a Polack keep his fly open?
In case he has to count to eleven.

* * *

O'Donald: You Polacks are all stupid.
Zabriski: That not true. We just like every-
      body else.
O'Donald: Okay, then. What's your name?
Zabriski: *Begins counting on fingers and
      then says*) "Stanley."
O'Donald: Stanley is not sixteen letters.
Zabriski: No . . . (*counting on fingers
      again*) "Happy birthday to you, Happy
      birthday to you . . ."

30

Mann Scharf, popular Hollywood publicist, makes this contribution: Grabowski and Molinski were walking down Eighth Avenue and met a priest who had his arm in a cast.

"How it happen?" asked Grabowski.

"I slipped in the bathtub and broke it," replied the father.

The two men continued their stroll and Grabowski said, "Hey, what is bathtub?"

"How I know," answered Molinski, "I not Catholic!"

* * *

Polish Martini: A marble in a glass of 7-Up.

* * *

How does one Polack find another Polack in the dark?
Wonderful.

How did the first 1,000 Polacks cross the ocean?
One swam across and the other 999 walked across on the dead fish.

* * *

Why can't Polacks eat dill pickles?
They can't get their heads in the jar.

* * *

How did the Polack get all those holes in his forehead?
Learning to eat with a fork.

* * *

Garbinski and Zywacki were sitting in a saloon, talking politics. "What would you do with Red China?" asked Garbinski.

"I'd put it on a purple tablecloth," replied Zywacki.

Jay Burton, scribe for Milton Berle, Carol Burnett and a host of other TV comics, swears this is the only Polish joke he ever wrote:

What is the capitol of Poland?

Forty Cents.

* * *

The four most dangerous people in the world:

A Jew with an attorney.

A Greek with sneakers.

A Frenchman with a jagged tooth.

A Polack with a credit card.

* * *

Zabiski: Hey, Custak, if you can tell me how many chickens I have in this bag, I give you both of them!

Custak: Three!

Zabiski: No fair! You looked in the bag!

A steel mill had a football game between the Poles and the Italians. They played all afternoon with neither team able to score. Suddenly, it was five o'clock, the factory whistle blew and the Italian team walked off the field. Three plays later, the Polacks scored a touchdown.

* * *

What do they call a swimming pool full of Polish girls?
Bay of Pigs.

* * *

Everyone knows that Cortez discovered Mexico and Columbus discovered America, but who discovered Poland?
The Roto Rooter man.

* * *

Polish Flag: Mop.

Lewis Wildman, Jersey City's greeting card king, tells about Pilzudski being a contestant on a television quiz show. "For $1,000," said the M.C., "tell us the meaning of Easter!"

Pilzudski paused for a moment and then said: "This man come out of ground . . ."

"That's it!" shouted the master of ceremonies. "You've won the thousand dollars!"

". . . And turns around," continued the Polack, "and if he see his shadow . . ."

* * *

Polish-Americans, offended by the viciousness of the jokes told about them, are quick to remind friends of the bravery of the Polish people during World War II.

The Poles are reputed to have barehandedly thrown sticks of dynamite into the hordes of attacking German soldiers. The Nazis then caught the sticks of dynamite, lit them, and threw them back.

Investment counselor Gary Judas tells about the Polish army sergeant who called his platoon to attention and shouted: "Men, after three week it be time to change underwear! Kozlow, you change with Banacek. Banacek you change with Linkowski. Linkowski you change with. . . ."

* * *

What do they call a Polack chasing a garbage truck?
A Galloping Gourmet.

* * *

Why did the Polack throw the clock out the window?
He wanted to see time fly.

Rancho Park golf pro, Ed Coleman, tells about the American, Frenchman and Pole in France who were sentenced to death on the guillotine. The judge said to the American, "Do you have any last words?" "Drop dead!" snapped the Yank. The judge signaled for the sentence to be carried out. The executioner pulled the lever and as the crowd gaped in astonishment, the giant blade came to a screeching halt three inches from severing the victim's head. "It is God's will," cried the astounded judge. "Let the American go free!"

They put the Frenchman on the block and the judge asked, "What are your final remarks?" "Go to hell!" the Frenchman shouted. Again the signal. The razor-sharp blade dropped and again it miraculously stopped only a quarter inch from the condemned prisoner's head. "It is the will of God," exclaimed the judge. "Set him free!"

Now they placed the Pole in position. "Before you are beheaded," said the judge, "do you have any last words?" "Yeah," said the Polack. "If you put a little grease in those grooves, blade comes down much easier!"

"... put a little grease in those grooves,
blade comes down much easier!"

Totie Fields got a scream with this on stage at the Riviera Hotel in Las Vegas:

Why does a Polack eat beans for dinner on Saturday night?

So he can take a bubble bath Sunday morning.

* * *

What does it say on the bottom of a Coke bottle in Poland?
Open other end.

* * *

Why does it take five Polacks to screw in a light bulb?
One to hold the light and four to turn the ladder.

* * *

Why is Santa Claus Polish?
Who else would wear a red suit?

How do you tell the property values in Poland?
The farther from Warsaw the more expensive.

* * *

Why does it take ten Polacks to hang a picture?
One to hold the nail and nine to push the wall.

* * *

Cyrankiewicz was having his eyes examined.
"Read the bottom line," said the optometrist.
"Hey," said the Polack, "I know that fellow!"

* * *

Polish homosexual walking down the street, carrying a midget under his arm. He meets another member of dubious sexuality and says, "Say, Arnold, want a drag before I throw him away?"

Polish woman was told by the doctor to come back the next day with a sample of her urine. She returned with a bedpan filled to the top.

"Mrs. Witkowski," admonished the physician, "How could you walk through the streets, carrying a bedpan full of urine!"

"What you mean *walk*," she replied, "I took bus!"

* * *

Los Angeles appliance tycoon Monte Mellman regales customers with the one about Zawadski the lumberjack who wanted to buy a saw. The clerk said, "This is our best model. It'll cut down fifty trees in six hours."

Zawadski bought it, but returned to the store next evening his face flushed with anger. "You cheat me," he complained. "You say this saw cut down fifty trees in six hour. I only cut thirty-five and it take me all day!"

The bewildered clerk took the cord attached to the saw and plugged it into an electric socket. He then pushed a button which started the motor. The Polack jumped back and shouted, "What be that noise?"

Mojalewski met his friend Sawicki on Third Avenue, laughing his head off. "Why you laugh?" asked Mojalewski.

"I think about dumbbell I see this morning," replied Sawicki.

"What you mean?" quizzed Mojalewski.

"This morning alarm clock forget to ring. Wife and I oversleep. It be after nine o'clock when I wake up. I jump into clothes without waking wife and just be ready to leave when bedroom door open. In come Iceman?"

"What you do?"

"I almost die laughing!"

"Why?" asked Mojalewski.

"It be so damn funny!" answered the Polack. "Can you imagine guy be so dumb, he comes into bedroom looking for icebox!"

* * *

How many Polacks does it take to make popcorn?
Twenty.
One to hold the pan and nineteen to shake the stove.

Savings and loan manager John Ekblad tells about the Cherokee chief who comes to California looking for a place to live. An unscrupulous real estate broker sells the Indian an outhouse.

Three days later, the agent drives by and sees a television antenna on the roof. A week later, he sees a second one.

"I notice you've got another TV antenna up on your roof," said the real estate man. "How come?"

"I rented out the basement to a Polack," replied the chief.

* * *

Potowski and Zablocki were working their first day in a coal mine. Potowski turned on his headlamp and said, "I bet you $5 you can't climb all the way up that beam of light."

"Oh, yes, I could," answered Zablocki.

"For $5 I say you can't."

"Five dollars I say I can!"

"Okay, go ahead and climb it."

"You can't fool me," said Zablocki. "I get halfway up and you'd turn the damn thing off!"

Polish Combat Soldier

Billy Barty, prince of the little people, tells about the two Polish astronauts who were circling the Earth in outer space. One of them was sent outside the capsule to walk around. An hour later he wanted to reenter, so he knocked on the door. The Polack inside said, "Who's there?"

* * *

Russia decided they wanted to have their own Disneyland. So they built a fence around Poland.

* * *

Polish underarm deodorant—Raid.

* * *

A young Polish girl was taking the state board examination to become a nurse. The doctor asked her, "How do you wash genitals?"

"The same way you wash Jews!" she replied innocently.

Phillip Moyer of El Modena, California tells about the lady who was showing a contractor through the second floor of her new house to advise him what colors to paint the rooms. "I'd like the bathroom done in white!"

The contractor walked over to the window and shouted: "Green up! Green up!"

"I want the bedroom in blue!" continued the woman.

The contractor yelled out the window, "Green up! Green up!"

"The halls should be done in beige!" Again the man barked out the window, "Green up! Green up!"

"Will you stop that!" ordered the woman angrily. "Every time I give you a color I want, you shout 'Green up!' What in God's name does that mean?"

"I'm terribly sorry, ma'am!" explained the contractor. "But I've got three Polacks down below putting in the lawn!"

* * *

Polish Cocktail: A mushroom in a glass of beer.

"What will you charge me to paint my house," asked the man of a Polish painter.

"Twelve dollar a day!" replied Bratkowski.

"Good Lord!" exclaimed the home owner. "I wouldn't pay Michelangelo that price!"

"I tell you one thing, by Joe," said the Polack, "if that Wop is doing job for less, he no be member of union!"

* * *

Shelley Graves, Grand Rapids, Michigan, tells about the three Polacks who were standing one on top of the other, trying to measure a flagpole.

A man passing by yelled up to them, "Why don't you take the pole, lay it down on the ground and measure it."

"We not want measure *length*," said the Polack in charge. "We want measure *height!*"

* * *

What's Polish surf and turf?
Herring and Kalbasi.

Theatrical rep, Ken Grayson, says it is a historical fact that Diogenes went all around the world carrying a lamp, trying to find an honest man. When he got to Poland, they stole his lamp.

* * *

Linkowski and Kawecki were driving from Detroit to Cleveland. Just outside the city limits they saw a sign: "Clean Rest Rooms." By the time they got to Cleveland they cleaned 147 rest rooms.

* * *

Financial adviser Steve Gerber asks: What happens when you cross a Jew with a Polack? You get a janitor who owns the building.

Giovani tells Polski that he passed the citizenship test by writing all the answers on the waistband of his undershorts.

Polski borrows Giovani's underwear and shows up the next day for the exam. He was the only one in the office, so the clerk decided to give him the test orally.

"How many original colonies were there in America?"

Polski, pretending he was thinking, faced about, turned over the waistband of his shorts and then answered, "34!"

The bewildered examiner figured the poor man was nervous and went on: "What are the colors of the flag?"

Again Polski checked his shorts and replied, "Brown and white!"

The public official decided to try one last question. "Who was the first president of the United States?"

The Polack glanced quickly at his undershorts and then proudly proclaimed:

"J. C. Penney!"

* * *

Did you hear about the . . .
—Two Polacks who hijacked a submarine and asked for a million dollars and two parachutes?

50

—Polack who went to a masquerade ball and at midnight when the hostess asked him to take off his mask, he said, "I ain't got one on!"

* * *

—Polack who shot an arrow in the air? Missed.

* * *

—Polish woman who had a hysterectomy so she'd stop having grandchildren?

* * *

—Polack who was two hours late because the escalator got stuck?

—Nervous Polish surgeon who was finally discharged from the hospital?
It wasn't so much all the patients he lost . . . it was those deep gashes he made in the operating table.

* * *

Did you hear about the . . .
—Polish woman who made her toilet into an end table?
She moved the sofa into the bathroom.

* * *

—Polack who stayed up all night studying for his urine test?

* * *

—Fleet-footed Polish girl?
She only ran after sailors.

—Polish nurse who drove right through a red light. A cop stopped her and said, "Don't you know what a red light stands for?" "Of course," said the nurse. "A bedpan! What else?"

* * *

Did you hear about the . . .
—Polack whose wife had triplets and he went out looking for the other two guys?

* * *

—Polish athlete at the Olympics who won a gold medal and went out and had it bronzed?

* * *

—Polack who invented the wheelbarrow so he could learn to walk on his hind legs?

—Polish farmer's daughter who suffered a fate worse than death to pay off the villain who held a mortgage on the family farm—and enjoyed it so much she went out looking for the guy who held the second mortgage?

* * *

Did you hear about the . . .
—Polack in the hotel who complained about the noise next door?
"I'm sorry, sir," said the desk clerk. "They're holding an Elks convention."
"I don't care if they've got him by the antlers," barked the Polack, "I wanna get some sleep!"

* * *

—Polish Kamikazi pilot who returned safely from forty missions?

—Polish prostitute who didn't vote? She
  didn't care who got in.

* * *

—Polish glass blower who inhaled?
  Now he's got a pane in the stomach.

* * *

Did you hear about the . . .
—Negro boys running toward their swimming
  hole, shouting, "The last one in is a dirty
  Polack!?"

* * *

—Polish race driver at Indianapolis who had
  to make seventy-five pit stops?
  Three for fuel.
  Four to change tires.
  And sixty-eight to ask directions.

—Polack who wouldn't go out with his wife because he found out she was married?

* * *

Did you hear about the . . .
—Polack who was asked if he'd like to become a Jehovah's Witness?
He said he couldn't because he didn't see the accident.

* * *

—Polish girl who thought a sanitary belt was a drink from a clean shot glass?

* * *

—Polack who smelled good only on one side? He didn't know where to buy any Left Guard.

56

—Polack who ordered a pizza?
He was asked if he wanted it cut into four or eight pieces. He said, "Make it four. I'll never be able to eat eight pieces."

* * *

Did you hear about the . . .
—Polish woman who shopped for three days looking for wheels for her miscarriage?

* * *

—Polack who thought Vat 69 was the pope's phone number?

* * *

—Polish housewife who got mad at her husband because he was off shooting craps and she didn't know how to cook them?

—Polish woman who wanted to turn in her
menstrual cycle for a Honda?

* * *

Did you hear about the . . .
—Polish plumber who looked at Niagara Falls
and said, "Give me time and I could fix it!"

* * *

—Polish efficiency expert who has all the boys
at the plant on their toes lately?
He raised the urinals twelve inches.

* * *

—Polack who saw a movie and then waited
four hours by the side door for the star to
come out?

—Polack who went up to a street-sprinkling truck and told the driver his car was leaking?

* * *

Did you hear about the . . .
—Polack who asked to be buried at sea? His son drowned trying to dig his grave.

* * *

—Polack who thought Peter Pan was something you put under your bed at night?

* * *

—Polish girl who lost her mind? For ten years she worked in a house of ill repute. Then she found out the rest of the girls got paid.

—Polack who took his pregnant wife to a supermarket because he heard that they had free delivery?

* * *

Did you hear about the . . .
—Polack who came home after being a prisoner of war for five years?
When he got off the plane a beautiful blonde walked up to him and said, "How'd you like to have something you haven't had in years?" And he said, "Don't tell me you've got a filter cigarette?"

* * *

—Polack who was so lazy he married a pregnant woman?

* * *

—Polack who hijacked an Israeli plane and demanded one million dollars in pledges?

Polish Brassiere

Did you hear about the . . .

—Polish girl who was so ugly that when she walked into a room the mice jumped up on chairs?

* * *

—Polack who went down to city hall for his driver's license?
It was so crowded he got in the wrong line. Now he's the only guy in the world married to a Toyota.

* * *

—Polish kidnapper who sent his hostage out to collect the ransom?

* * *

—Polish pickpocket who only has one finger? He steals nothing but key rings.

—Polack who was so bowlegged he could walk down a bowling alley while the game was going on?

* * *

Did you hear about the . . .
—Polack who opened up a travel agency and went broke in two weeks?
He kept trying to book reservations on the *Titanic, Lusitania* and the *Andrea Dorea.*

* * *

—Polish parachute?
It opens on impact.

* * *

—Polish hemophiliac who tried to cure himself with acupuncture?

—Polish coyote that chewed off three legs and he was still caught in the trap?

* * *

Did you hear about the . . .
—Twelve Polish astronauts who died in the line of duty?
They couldn't get a strong enough sling-shot.

* * *

—Polish stripper who had such a free-swinging figure when she ran off stage she started her own applause?

* * *

—Polack who gave his wife a 300-piece dinner set for Christmas?
It was only supposed to be twenty-four pieces but he tripped coming home from the store.

—Polack who suffers from insomnia?
Keeps waking up every few days.

* * *

Did you hear about the . . .
—Polack who had a pair of water skis he
never got to use?
He couldn't find a lake on a hill.

* * *

—Polish orchestra that stopped in the middle
of a performance to clean the saliva out of
their instruments?
It was a string orchestra.

* * *

Polish fairy who was so ugly he had to go
out with girls?

Polack who ran around the cereal box because it said: "Tear around the top!"

* * *

Did you hear about the . . .
Polish accountant?
He absconded with the accounts payable.

* * *

—Ugly Polish stripper who worked in a nudie show?
Everybody'd yell, "Put it on! Put it on!"

* * *

—Polack who was so dumb he thought manual labor was the president of Mexico?

—Polack who got married so many times, he married one of his former wives again and didn't even know it?
He never would have found it out except he recognized his mother-in-law!

* * *

Did you hear about the . . .
—Polack who was twenty-two years old before he knew which part of the olive to throw away?

* * *

—Polack who went to a carnival and saw a man having an epileptic fit and jumped on him?
He thought it was a new ride.

* * *

—Polish auto mechanic who went to a psychiatrist and insisted on lying under the couch?

—Polish girl whose bags under her eyes were so big, her nose looked like it was wearing a saddle?

* * *

Did you hear about the . . .
—Polack who stepped in a pile of cow dung and started crying?
He thought he was melting.

* * *

—High class Polish girl who only had her number written in telephone booths on the east side of town?

* * *

—Polish airliner that crashed?
It ran out of coal.

Did you hear about the . . .
—Polish girl who took a job as a model in Alaska?
She poses for totem poles.

* * *

—Polish street cleaner who went berserk following a merry-go-round?

* * *

—Polish girl who was so bowlegged she looked like one bite out of a doughnut?

* * *

—Polack who kept laughing when they put him in the electric chair?
He said, "The joke's on you. You've got the wrong guy!"

—Polish girl who couldn't understand why she was blessed with twins, since she had never been on a double date?

* * *

—Polack who told his wife to get something on the TV set?
So she went out and hocked it.

* * *

—Three-fingered Polish pickpocket?
He only steals bowling balls.

* * *

—Polish surgeon who worked in a doughnut factory?
He made the incision then someone else put the jelly in.

Did you hear about the . . .
—Polish cop who gave out twenty-two parking tickets before he found out he was in a drive-in movie?

* * *

—Polack who hates dogs?
He went to a masquerade ball as a lamp post.

* * *

—Polish plumber's daughter?
Every time someone told her a spicy joke her cheeks flushed.

* * *

Did you hear about the . . .
—Polish coal miner who takes a bath just once a week?
Then he bottles the bath water and sells it for ink.

—Polish girl everybody thought was such a
happy kid because she was always smiling?
Then they found out her false teeth were too
big.

* * *

—Polack who couldn't count to ten?
One of his fingers was missing.

* * *

—Polish girl who never wore a necklace?
She just braided her wrinkles.

* * *

GAWOOMPKI

How many Polacks does it take to make love?
Three.
Two to do it and one to read the instructions
out of the book.

* * *

Why did the Polack stop at the house of ill repute?
He was waiting for the light to change.

* * *

What happened when they dropped the Atom
Bomb on Warsaw?
It did $10.15 worth of damage.

* * *

How does a Polish mother put on her child's
underwear?
Yellow in front, brown in back.

Polish Sex Manual

Why are Polish mothers so strong and square-shouldered?
From raising dumbbells.

* * *

What's harder than getting six pregnant Polish women in a Volkswagen?
Getting six Polish women pregnant in a Volkswagen.

* * *

Two Secretaries at Lunch:
Gloria: I was raped last night by a Polack.
Helen: How do you know he was Polish?
Gloria: I had to help him.

* * *

Polish couple had a double ring ceremony. They were married in a bathtub.

The Morning After:

Italian Girl: My mother would die if she found out.

Spanish Girl: Now I will love you always.

Russian Girl: My body belongs to you; my soul will always belong to the state!

German Girl: After we go to beer garden, yah?

Swedish Girl: Aye tank aye go home now.

French Girl: For this I get a new dress, oui?

Chinese Girl: Now you know it's not true.

English Girl: Rather pleasant, what?

American Girl: Damn, I must've been really crocked. What'd you say your name was?

Jewish Girl: I'll have to go to the beauty parlor today!

Polish Girl: Can you really get me a screen test?

* * *

A Madison Avenue advertising agency conducted a survey in Europe to find out which was the most popular feminine hygiene spray. They discovered that in France it was a product called "Feminique." In England, it was "Pristine." And in Poland, it was "Janitor in a Drum."

Polish Wedding Good Luck Guide for the Bride:

    Something old,
    Something new,
    Something borrowed,
    Something blue.
    Something red,
    Something orange,
    Something purple,
    Something . . .

* * *

How Can You Tell the Groom at a Polish Wedding?
—He's the one with the dirty T-shirt.

* * *

—He's the one with the white bowling shoes.

* * *

—He's the one not wearing a bowling shirt.

* * *

—He's the one wearing a tuxedo and combat boots.

Two Poles Walking Abreast

How can you tell the bride at a Polish wedding?
She's the one with the braided armpits and sequins on her sneakers.

* * *

When Sophie returned from her honeymoon, she telephoned the doctor. "Those birth control pills you gave me aren't working!"

"What do you mean, not working?" asked the surprised physician. "I just gave them to you a week ago!"

"Well," replied the newlywed. "They keep falling out!"

* * *

How can you tell the mother-in-law at a Polish wedding?
She's the one on her hands and knees picking up the rice.

After making violent love to his wife for over an hour, Wladislaw said to her, "Why the hell did I ever marry you! You've got nothing on top . . . nothing on bottom . . ."

"Look," she gasped. "Get off my back!"

* * *

Ernie Medwig of Pittsburgh tells about Prapowski coming home and finding his wife in bed with another man. The Pole took out a gun from the drawer and put it to his head. The wife's lover jumped up and shouted, "Hey, what're you doing?"

"Shut up!" said the Polack. "You're next!"

* * *

What brings tears to a Polish mother's eyes? When she buys her son his first athletic supporter.

Jack Stokes, Southern California golf pro, always gets a big laugh with this one: Zimbriski and Raczkiewicz were hunting game out in the woods. Suddenly they came across a stark-naked blonde sitting on a tree stump.

"Hey," shouted Zimbriski. "Are you game?"

"Yes!" replied the woman.

So he shot her.

* * *

Rafael Vega, of Casa Vega, the great Sherman Oaks Mexican eatery, provided this gem: An obstetrician called on Mrs. Sobieski two days after she had delivered a husky youngster and found her holding an ice bag to her bosom.

"Trouble with your breasts?" asked the M.D.

"No trouble, doctor," replied the woman. "I do this to keep milk fresh!"

Polish Peeping Tom

"How's your wife?" asked Cusick.

"She's up in bed with laryngitis," replied Novack.

"Oh," retorted his friend. "Is that Greek bastard around again!"

* * *

Bridegroom to the hotel clerk, "How much do we owe for the room?"

"Five bucks apiece!"

Smolinski handed him fifty dollars.

* * *

Have you heard about the sixty-second Polish sex maniac?

Got a minute?

* * *

Cad: A Polack who doesn't tell his wife he's sterile until after she's pregnant.

86

Talent manager Arnold Mills tells about the love-sick Romeo who went to a doctor and said, "I'm dating a Polish girl and so I want to become a Pole!"

"That's a little unusual," said the dumb-founded physician. "But if that's what you want, okay. In order to become a real Polack I'll have to remove half your brain!"

"I'll do it!" agreed the young lover.

After the operation, the doctor revived his patient and said, "I'm terribly sorry! By mistake, I removed three-quarters of your brain!"

"Oh, mama, mia!" shouted the bewildered boy.

* * *

Chicago exec sec Sandy Bylczynski tells about the Polish couple who planned to get married and went to the doctor for their blood test. The M.D. then tried to explain sex to them. The boy just listened with a dumb expression on his face.

So the doctor took his fiancée over to the examination table, had her lie down and then made love to her. "Now do you understand?" asked the physician.

"Yeah," said the Polack. "But how often do I have to bring her in?"

Miss Konarski walked into a bank, carrying a large paper bag filled with nickels, dimes and quarters. "Did you hoard all this money by yourself?" inquired the teller.

"No," said the girl. "My sister whored half of it!"

* * *

Skiing: A Polish Love-In.

* * *

Private Polachek, of the Foreign Legion, hadn't seen a woman in years. "I'm getting pretty frustrated," said the Legionnaire to his sergeant. "What am I going to do?"

"See that camel over there," answered the NCO. "The men are supposed to use that animal when they need to relieve themselves!"

That night the sergeant was awakened by the camel squealing and screeching. He discovered Polachek kissing and hugging the animal and having a great time.

"What're you doing?" shouted the sergeant. "You're supposed to take the camel and ride it into town where all the women are!"

What do they call a stork that delivers Polish babies?
A dope peddler.

* * *

Polish marriage proposal: "You're gonna have a *what?*"

* * *

While selling construction equipment, Bob Bernard tells this one: Mayor Lindsay declared war on the rats in New York. His Honor ordered the health inspector to send nine Polish exterminators down into the sewers to wipe out the rodents.

A month later, only six of the nine Poles came back. "What happened to the other three men?" demanded the mayor.

"They defected to the enemy!" exclaimed the inspector. "And out of the six that returned, two brought back war brides!"

How can you tell which kid in the first grade class is Polish?
The one with the rusty zipper and the yellow sneakers.

* * *

Why did the Polish kids stop playing in the sandbox?
The cats kept trying to bury them.

* * *

Real estate broker Carol Malouf (who is Lebanese) tells about the Polish Captain in London during World War II. He picked up a streetwalker and took her out to dinner. They went back to her apartment and had a wonderful evening.

Next morning she fixed him breakfast, helped him on with his boots, and as he walked out the door, she shouted, "Hey, dearie! What about money?"

"Madam!" said the Captain with a flourish. "A Polish officer never accepts money!"

How do Polacks reproduce?
They exchange underwear.

* * *

A Polish girl was walking down Main Street with a pig under her arm. She met a girl friend who said, "Where did you get the pig?"

And the pig said, "I won her in a raffle!"

* * *

Miami attorney Arthur Davis likes the one about the Pole whose wife had just given birth. When the nurse brought the news, he took it very casually. She decided to shake him up a bit and brought a black baby.

"What do you think of your new son?" she asked.

"Cute little cheeks," replied the new father. "Tight hair! Real nice!"

"Aren't you surprised that it's black?" questioned the astonished nurse.

"Heck no!" said the Polack. "My wife burn everything!"

Have you heard about the new Polish under-arm deodorant?
It's called: No Bugs My Lady.

* * *

What happens when you give a Polish hooker a quarter?
You get double green stamps and twenty-four cents change.

* * *

Lloyd Gaynes, ABC-TV West Coast director of daytime programming, tells about the Polish couple in a motel. A sex maniac crashed into their room and at gunpoint forced the husband out of bed.

He drew a circle on the floor with a piece of chalk, and then said to him, "Stand in that circle. If you move out of it, I'll kill you!"

The intruder hopped in bed with the Pole's wife, made love to her for over an hour and then left. "My god!" cried the distraught woman. "Why didn't you do something?"

"I did," said the Polack. "I jumped out of the circle three times!"

What's the difference between a Polish wedding and a Polish funeral?
One less drunk.

* * *

Polish Lipstick: Preparation H.

* * *

A Polish couple got married and on their wedding night checked into a motel. They got themselves settled and in a few moments she called, "How about it, Chet?"

There was no answer. An hour later she repeated the question: "Chet, how about it?"

Still no answer. Soon it got to be five in the morning and by then she was fuming. "Chet, how about it?"

Finally he answered, "How about what?"

"How about going to sleep?" she replied.

Why don't Polish mothers like to breastfeed their children?
It hurts too much when they boil their nipples.

* * *

What do they call a Polish prostitute?
A ski jump.

* * *

TV director Bill Darcy tells about the groom at a Polish wedding. The ceremony had taken place in the ballroom of the town hotel. The newly married husband came down from the bridal suite and said to a buddy, "My best friend be upstairs in bed with my wife!"

"What are you going to do about it?" asked his pal.

"Nothing," replied the Polack. "He so drunk he thinks he be me!"

Novack: I came home yesterday and found stranger making love to my wife.
Cusick: What you do?
Novack: I fix him. I threw his umbrella out window and pray for rain.

* * *

Why did the bride think she had the most posh Polish wedding in Poland?
Her veil practically covered her overalls.

* * *

Witkowski got into the mine elevator, chuckling out loud.

"What's the joke?" asked the foreman.

"I sure have big laugh on Jancywicz," replied the Polack. "I just find out he pay my wife five dollars to kiss her and I do it for nothing!"

Miss Luzinski was driving along the highway when a police car stopped her. The cop said, "Why don't you have a red light on this car?"

"It ain't that kind of a car!" she answered with a smile.

* * *

Television and motion picture scribe, Brad Radnitz, tells about the girl who, against her family's wishes, ran off and married a Polack. The eloping bride received the following telegram from her parents:

"DO *NOT* COME HOME AND ALL WILL BE FORGIVEN."

* * *

Miss Kozcynski sat opposite a man on a desolate train, looking sad and lonely. He read his magazines for awhile and then said, "Excuse me, Miss! Would you like to take a look at my *Cosmopolitan?*"

"Mister!" said the Polish girl. "If you dare try, I'll scream!"

Middle-aged Wojeck and Rojeck were sitting in a saloon discussing their past lives. "I've lived a good life." said Wojeck. "There's only one thing I could be ashamed of. My mother once caught me in a very embarrassing act!"

"'Don't worry about it," soothed Rojeck. "All us kids did that!"

"I know," said Wojeck. "But it was only yesterday that she caught me!"

* * *

Why do Polish women wear veils when they get married?
To keep the flies off their faces.

* * *

Novack: I come home last night and find some strange guy kissing my wife.
Cusick: Holy smoke! What you do?
Novack: Ha! Ha! I fix them. I shut off lights so they not see what they were doing.

Comedy writer Ray Parker tells about the Polish teenagers who came home from their honeymoon. The next day the bridegroom found his wife in the kitchen crying.

"What's the matter, honey?" he inquired.

"I rinsed the ice cubes in this hot water and now I can't find them," she explained tearfully.

* * *

Sophie: I never met you before but I've heard plenty about your lovemaking.
Zeke: Oh, it be nothing.
Sophie: That's what I heard.

* * *

Prisoner Pozinski serving a twenty-year sentence in a Michigan jail was reminiscing with a fellow inmate about his wife.

"We used to have such fun at the seaside burying each other in the soft, white sand!"

"Must've been nice!" said his cellmate.

"Yeah," said the Polack, "When I get out, I think I go back and dig her up!"

Adam and Eve must have been the first Polacks. They didn't have any clothes, all they had to eat was an apple, and they thought they were living in Paradise.

* * *

Drakich and Wishnak are sipping a beer at the neighborhood gin mill. "What have you be doing today?" asked Drakich.

"I be laying linoleum," replied Wishnak.

"Has she got a friend?" said Drakich.

* * *

Polish Love Song: "She was going to have her face lifted but she didn't have the Jack."

* * *

Witkowski suspected his wife of cheating.

One day he rushed into the apartment unexpectedly and shot the two occupants dead. Then he looked around and said, "Hey, this is the wrong apartment."

Kazewski and Giordano agreed to a bet on who could make love to his wife more times in one night. They took adjoining hotel rooms and decided that each time they did they would carve a notch on the wall.

Giordano performed once at ten o'clock, placing a scratch on the wall. Then at two A.M. he drew another gash. By six o'clock he had three scratches.

At eight in the morning, the Polack came in and looked at the marks. "My god! One hundred and eleven!" cried Kazewski. "He beat me by three!"

* * *

Farmers Dumbrowski and Kadlubek met in town:

Dumbrowski: I'm married twenty-five year today.

Kadlubek: Congratulations!

Dumbrowski: What you think? My wife told me to kill a chicken to celebrate, but I didn't.

Kadlubek: How come?

Dumbrowski: Why take it out on a chicken for something that happencd twenty-five years ago.

Giant Polish dock worker, Kraczewski, was considered by most of the longshoremen to be a great lover. They claimed he could make love to twenty girls in an hour. When some disbelieving seamen showed up, bets were made, and the next night twenty girls were lined up in one of the warehouses.

The big Polack went to work. He made love to the first dozen, when suddenly he fell to the floor in a state of exhaustion.

His pals rushed up to him, screaming, "What happened?"

"I dunno," answered Kraczewski. "I did okay this afternoon at rehearsal!"

* * *

KOLACHKI

What do you get when you cross a midget with a Polack?
A short garbage man.

* * *

"Do you know how to save a Polack?"
"No!"
"That's good!"

* * *

Brain Tumor: Pimple on a Polack's behind.

* * *

Dave Traurig, Sales Director for the Sheraton Hotels and motor inns, tells about Sladowski and Wiznecki getting a job in a factory. The first day there, Wiznecki climbed up on a ladder, stretched out his arms and shouted: "I'm a light! I'm a light!"

"What the hell are you doing?" asked the boss.

"I'm a light!" answered Wiznecki.

"Get down from there!" ordered the owner. "Do that again and you're fired!"

Soon as he walked away Wiznecki got up on the ladder again and with outstretched arms exclaimed: "I'm a light! I'm a light!"

"Okay, you're fired!" declared his employer.

The Pole started walking out of the plant when his friend, Sladowski, joined him. "Where the hell are you going?" asked the bewildered boss.

"I'm leaving!" replied the Polack indignantly. "I no work in place where there no be lights!"

* * *

And what about the Polack who hijacked a train to Cuba?

What does XXX stand for?
Three Polacks co-signing a note.

* * *

Polish Car Pool: Eight Polacks carrying a Volkswagen to work.

* * *

Barbi McCulloch tells about the Polack and the two Mexicans who were to be hung in Texas for rustling. The lynch mob brought the three men to a tree at the edge of the Rio Grande. The idea was that after each man died, they'd cut the rope and he'd drift down the river out of sight.

They put the first Mexican in the noose, but he was so greasy he slipped out, fell into the river, and swam away to freedom.

They tied the noose around the second Mexican's head. He, too, oozed out of the rope, dropped into the river and escaped.

Then as they dragged the Polack toward the scaffold he said: "Could you make the noose a little tighter—I can't swim!"

How to Tie Your Shoes—the Polish Way

Mort Fleischmann, RCA's West Coast director of news and information, contributed this gem:

Ziwacki bought a new car and after he left the showroom decided to catch a movie. When he came out, Ziwacki noticed he'd locked the car and left the keys in the ignition.

Ziwacki telephoned the dealer. "Which is cheapest window to break?"

"You don't have to break any of the windows," explained the auto seller. "I'll come right down with another key and we can open it together!"

"No! No!" shouted the Polack. "I got to know right now. It be going to rain and I want to put top up!"

* * *

What did the Polish airplane manufacturers do before the airplane was invented?

They made parachutes.

"We must have done something to offend Mrs. Polanski, our neighbor," said Mrs. Brown to her husband. "She hasn't been over for several days."

"Be sure to find out what it is when she does come over," said Mr. Brown, "so we can do it again!"

* * *

Vocal groups booker Bonnie Larson tells about Dumbrowski and Moronski, who are out hunting and kill a deer. They each grabbed a hind leg and began pulling it toward their truck. But the antlers kept slowing them down.

Another hunter, passing by, said, "Why don't you pull that thing by the horns!" They did.

Two hours later, Dumbrowski said, "This be good idea. It be lot easier!"

"Yeah," said Moronski. "But we be getting further and further away from the truck!"

How do you get a Polack out of a tub of water?

Throw in a bar of soap.

* * *

Miami philosopher Sid Danoff likes the one about the two Polacks who buy a truckload of watermelons for a buck apiece.

They sell every one of them for a dollar each. After counting up their money they realize they've got the same amount they spent.

"See," said one of the Polacks, "I told you we shoulda got a bigger truck!"

* * *

How did the Polack spell "farm"?
"E yi e yi yo."

* * *

What is the Polish national anthem?
Hymn to the Roto Rooter man.

What does it mean when you see an orange
sewer plate on the street?
A Polish Howard Johnson's.

* * *

They just announced for the first time in history a new medical development in Poland.
They performed the first transplant of a human
appendix.

* * *

Dana Blatt of Encino asks: Why do Polacks
make the best astronauts?
Because they took up space in school.

* * *

What do we do with our old sanitation trucks?
We send them to Poland and sell them as used
campers.

Comedian-actor-writer Howard Storm came up with this pearl: What do goods made in Poland have stamped on them?
Untouched by human hands.

* * *

Why do Polacks make bad sky divers?
They miss the earth.

* * *

What happened to the Polish polo team?
The horses drowned.

* * *

Dave Levin, the storytelling sandwich sculptor of Art's Delicatessen in Studio City, entertains customers with this one: What did the Polish prostitute give her daughter for a birthday present?
Everything west of Broadway.

Poles indignant over the rash of jokes degrading every aspect of their culture, decided to prove to the world that they could make a significant contribution to society. They held a beauty contest in Poland. Nobody won.

* * *

Why don't you ever hear about Polacks committing suicide?
They can't get killed jumping out of a basement window!

* * *

What is a Polish seven-course dinner?
A pound of baloney and a six-pack.

* * *

Why are there more blacks in Chicago than Poles in Detroit?
Chicago had first choice.

Why do they only have two pallbearers at a Polish funeral?
Because a garbage can only has two handles.

Definition of a Maniac: A Polack in a bawdy house with a credit card.

* * *

Marie Ferrell of New Jersey says she felt awful when the American track team showed up late for their event at the Munich Olympics. The boys didn't know their starting time had been changed. But what about the poor Polish team. They showed up in Mexico City.

* * *

Sid Weksler, California frozen egg king, asks: Why does it take a Polack five days to wash his basement windows?
He needs four and a half days to dig the holes for the ladder.

Professor Potacki conducted an experiment to show how a frog reacted to human stimulus. The scientist explained: "At first the frog jumped sixteen feet. When I cut off one leg, I established that a three-legged frog could only jump twelve feet. I cut off another leg and yelled, 'Jump!' I concluded that a two-legged frog could only jump nine feet!"

"I then found that the frog with one leg could jump only six feet. I cut off the last leg, shouted, 'Jump!' and the frog didn't move. So therefore I concluded that a frog with no legs is deaf!"

* * *

Who was Alexander Graham Polowski?
The first telephone Pole.

* * *

UCLA co-ed Libby Getz asks: What is the *second* stupidest thing in the world?
A Polack out in the middle of the ocean, trying to build a foundation for a house.

What is the *stupidest* thing in the world?
An Italian trying to build a house on the foundation.

* * *

What is the easiest job in Poland?
Intelligence officer in the Polish army.

* * *

Custak walked into a lumber camp in Oregon and said to the man in charge, "I want to cut wood with you guys here in the north woods!" "You're nuts!" said the head lumberjack. "You're only five feet tall. You don't weigh more than a hundred pounds, soaking-wet. Besides, what kind of experience do you have to be a lumberjack?"

"The Sahara Forest!" replied the bold Polack.

In what section of the newspaper do they print Polish obituaries?
Under *Civic Improvements*.

* * *

There is a contest that has $2.00 for the first prize. The second prize is a trip to Poland.

* * *

A tux-clad comedian, performing at Gene Penoz' Moose Club in Pittsburgh, was stunned momentarily after he asked: "What's black and white and floats down the river on its back?"

"The next comedian who tells a Polish joke," shouted a member of the audience.

* * *

What do you get when you cross a Polack and a flower?
A blooming idiot.

If there are thirty motorcycles going down the street, how can you tell which one the Polack is on?
It's the one with the training wheels.

* * *

Russia claims they could have the world's largest zoo. All they have to do is build a fence around Poland.

* * *

What's the first thing a Polack does when he gets out of the shower?
Takes off his clothes.

* * *

Why do Polish men have pierced elbows?
So they can wear cuff links in the summer!

Harry and Fred had been playing golf for twenty-five years and for twenty-five years Fred had lost to his pal. Fred decided to find the greatest partner to help him beat Harry. So he got this giant Polish steelworker.

They were out on the first tee, the hole was 501 yards. The Polack hit a tremendous drive and the ball landed on the green—a 501-yard smash.

"I can't beat this guy," moaned Harry. "He'll probably go two on every hole. Here's the money. Incidentally, how does he putt?"

"Same way he drives," said Fred, walking toward the club house.

* * *

For years the Russians have maintained that they invented almost every gadget or mechanical device known to man.

Though most of their claims have been disputed, even the Russians are willing to admit that the Polacks invented the limbo dance.

It came about quite by accident. They were trying to squeeze under the door of a pay toilet.

How do you know when a Polack has died? All the garbage trucks have their lights on.

* * *

Singing star, Burt Taylor, tells about Polski at the airport trying to get back to Poland. The ticket cost $200. He only had $199.95. The Pole ran around stopping people to scrape up the nickel.

Finally, he cornered a well-dressed business executive and said, "Mister, you lend me nickel?"

"Leave me alone," said the man.

"Please," begged Polski. "I need five cents to go back to Poland."

"Oh, here's a quarter, then," said the man, "Take four more with you!"

On the UCLA campus, Mike Bols tells about Karpinski trying to join a fraternity up at Washington State. The boys didn't want him. They told him in order to be accepted, he'd have to do three things: Drink a gallon of homemade liquor, kill a grizzly bear and rape an Eskimo woman.

The Polish student guzzled down the booze and then staggered off into the woods. He returned the next day, his clothes tattered and torn. "What happened?" asked the frat brothers.

"Never mind!" retorted the boy. "Where's that Eskimo woman you want me to kill!"

* * *

What do they call a pig in a blanket?
A Polish prostitute.

* * *

Mack: Do you know how to speak Polish?
Jack: No!
Mack: How does it feel to be dumber than a Polack?

What do they call a Polack who sits in a tree?
A branch manager.

* * *

Larry Yeston, Lerner shops exec, recalls the one about the Negro jumping up and down on a manhole cover, shouting, "49! 49! 49!"

Along came Kuloc. "What you do?" he said.

"Here man," said the black, "you jump for awhile!"

Kuloc began leaping up and down on the manhole cover. Suddenly, the black snatched the cover away and the Polack fell into the sewer.

The colored man replaced it and, jumping up and down, shouted, "50! 50! 50!"

* * *

Who wears a polka dot tie, an outrageously striped vest and checkered pants, and sits on a wall?
Humpty Dumbrowski.

Sharalee Beard, with the Johnny Mann Singers, tells about the man who walked into a cannibal butcher shop to buy a pound of brains. There were three piles. $1 a pound, $10 a pound, and $10,000 a pound.

"Why is the first pile only a dollar?" asked the customer.

"Those are white people's brains!" answered the cannibal proprietor.

"How come the second bunch is $10?"

"Those are Negro brains," said the owner.

"Why is the other pile $10,000?"

"They're Polish brains!" explained the boss.

"But why are they so expensive?"

"Do you know how many Polacks we have to kill to get a pound of brains?"

* * *

How many Polacks does it take to pull off a kidnapping?
Six.
One to kidnap the victim and five to write the ransom note.

In Las Vegas, TV's Don Adams tells about the Indian (from Bombay), the Jew, and the Polack, who are stuck out in the country in a storm. They came to a farm house and asked to be put up for the night.

"I have a small cabin in back, but there's only room for two," said the farmer. "One of you will have to sleep in the barn."

The Indian volunteered. Five minutes later, he knocked on the cabin door and said to his Polish and Jewish friends, "I can't stay in the barn. There is a cow there and that is against my religion."

"That's all right," said the Jew. "I'll sleep in the barn."

Five minutes later, there was knock on the cabin door and the Jew said, "I'm sorry, there's a pig in the barn. That's against my religion."

"That's okay," said the Polack. "I'll sleep in the barn!"

Five minutes later, there was a knock on the door. The Indian and the Jew opened it and there stood the pig and the cow.

* * *

Little Davie Blumenfield from Atlantic City asks: What's a Polish pencil?
A pencil with an eraser on both ends.

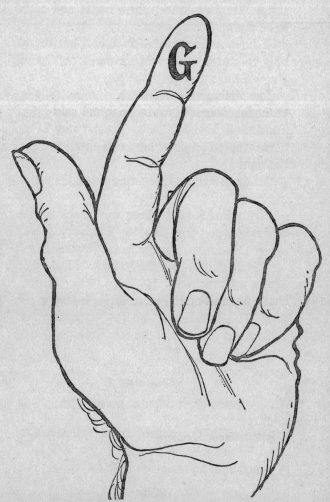

Polish Handkerhief, Monogrammed

What's a Polish Mai-Tai?
Eight Polacks standing around drinking
through straws from a septic tank.

* * *

Comedian-cruise director, Tony Noice,
writes that this is a howl among the ship's pas-
sengers:
What is the toughest job in Hamtramck,
Michigan?
Riding shotgun on the garbage truck.

* * *

What's a Garachski?
That's what a Polack opens his garage with.

* * *

What was the most popular horror film in Poland?
"The Unsmellable Man."

Miss Pontiatowski was arrested in a department store for shoplifting. They got suspicious when she wore the same maternity dress fourteen months in a row.

When the house detective shook her, she immediately gave birth to a drip-dry wedding gown, a tube of tooth paste, a mop handle and a television set.

* * *

Real estate broker Jackie Peters tells about Kachowski and Wlasowich getting drunk and stumbling into an Irish wake. They were so polluted they couldn't even find the corpse. But for ten minutes they stood in front of a grand piano.

Finally, Kachowski nudged his friend and said, "Do you recognize him?"

"Hell, no!" slobbered Wlasowich. "But he sure has a great set of teeth!"

Who has a beard, wears a dirty white robe and
rides a pig?
Lawrence of Poland.

During a recent stock market dip, a broker lost everything. "I have no money to pay you, Mr. Kluzewski," he said to the plumber, who had just presented a large bill. "In lieu of payment will you take a Rembrandt?"

"If it has four good tires," said the Polack, "you got a deal!"

* * *

How can you tell a Polack from a monkey? The monkey peels the banana before eating it.

* * *

Ted Sawaski, Rialto, California, insurance agent, tells about Stanislaw Putsidwakim going to court to have his name changed.

"I can understand how you feel," sympathized the judge. "A name like Stanislaw Putsidwakim could certainly be a handicap. What would you like to change it to?"

"*George* Putsidwakim," said the Polack.

One night on his TV show Joey Bishop broke up the audience with: "The other day I was in a town so small the head of the Mafia was Polish."

* * *

Why is a Polish postman like an ape?
Cause his feet smell like the inside of a gorilla's stomach.

* * *

They put an Indian on a nickel—now they're going to put a Polack on a slug.

* * *

Stanley and his girl friend were sitting in the park. Suddenly, a police car whizzed by with its siren going full blast. "Listen, darling," cooed the girl, "they're playing our song!"

Wiznecki got an out of town construction job and asked his pal, Boleslaw, to check up on his wife to see that she didn't fool around with anybody.

Six months later he returned and found his spouse and his buddy in bed doing the very thing he tried to avoid. Wiznecki called his wife every name in the book and then threatened divorce.

"And as for you, you dirty dog," the Polack shouted at his best friend, "couldn't you at least stop while I'm talking to you!"

* * *

Polish girl received a letter from her boyfriend in the army with a bunch of Xs on the bottom. "The dirty rat," she muttered. "I'll teach him to double-cross me!"

* * *

Polish Proverb: If ignorance was commercial we'd all be millionaires.

Bob Feldman of Acme Vending likes the one about the Pole, the black, and the Mexican, who were out of work and living together. The Polack came home one night and announced he had gotten a job. "Hey, fellas, wake me up tomorrow morning at six," he said, "I have to be at work by 6:30!"

While the Polack slept, the black said to the Mexican, "He got a job because he's white. We can't get one because we're brown and black." So during the night they put shoe black all over the Polack. Then they agreed to wake him late.

Next morning, when the Polish boy arrived at work, the foreman said, "Who are you?"

"You hired me yesterday," he replied. "You told me to be here at 6:30!"

"I hired a white man—you're black."

"I am not!"

"Yes you are! Go look in the mirror!"

The Polack rushed over to a mirror, looked at himself and exclaimed, "My God! They woke up the wrong one!"

Wysotski and Voytek went to a lumber yard. Wysotski waited in the car while Voytek spoke to the foreman. "I want some 3x4's!" said Voytek.

"We've only got 2x4's!" said the lumber man.

"Wait, I go ask my partner!" Voytek returned and said "Okay."

"How long do you want them?" asked the foreman.

"Just a minute, I go check with my partner!" Voytek came back in a few seconds and said, "We'll want them for a while—we building a house!"

* * *

Do you know how Polacks make babies?
No.
Boy, are you dumb!

* * *

Why do Polacks wear turtleneck sweaters?
To hide their flea collars.

Zaleski and Gornicki were riding in the country when their car broke down. "How far is it back to Detroit?" asked Zaleski of a service station attendant.

"Twenty miles," he replied.

"We'd better get going," said Gornicki. "Twenty miles is a long way to walk!"

"That's not so much!" answered Zaleski. "It's only ten miles apiece!"

* * *

"What you doin'?" asked Ladislas.

"I write letter to myself," answered Sigismund.

"What you tell yourself?"

"How do I know?" snapped Sigismund. "I no get letter until tomorrow!"

Wojawicz and Slovak were placed in a padded cell. Wojawicz kept trying to hammer a nail into the wall. But he had the head of the nail against the wall and was hammering on the pointed end.

"I'm supposed to be nuts," he says to his friend, "but the nails they give you here have the pointed end on the wrong side."

"You're crazy, all right," says Slovak. "That nail is for the other wall!"

* * *

Zuchva and Koszyczki lived together, and one night Zuchva came home and found Koszyczki walking around the apartment without any clothes on except for a high top hat.

"Why you walk around house without clothes on?" asked Zuchva.

"It make no difference," answered Koszyczki. "Nobody ever come here to see us."

"Then why you wear high top hat?"

"Somebody might!"

* * *

ABOUT THE AUTHOR

Larry Wilde is the world's most popular jester in print. With sales of over 4 million copies, Larry has become the largest selling jokesmith in publishing history.

Mr. Wilde's literary contribution to the comedic field also includes two serious books considered to be definitive works on the subject of humor: *The Great Comedians* and *How The Great Comedy Writers Create Laughter*. He has also published *The Complete Book of Ethnic Humor*, the first comprehensive assortment of jokes characterizing America's mirth-loving minorities.

Larry Wilde is a twenty-five-year show business veteran, having served as a comedian, actor, writer, performer, and producer. He has appeared in the nation's finest clubs and hotels, and on television in commercials, as well as sitcoms like *Mary Tyler Moore, Rhoda, Sanford and Son,* and many others.

Mr. Wilde and his wife, Maryruth, reside in Los Angeles where he continues to write, perform, act, and lecture on the subject of comedy.

LAUGH ALONG WITH
Larry Wilde

"America's bestselling humorist."
—The New York Times

V
by A.C. Crispin
☐ 42237-7/$2.95   ☐ 43231-3/$3.50 (in Canada)
V: EAST COAST CRISIS
by Howard Weinstein and A.C. Crispin
☐ 42259-8/$2.95   ☐ 43251-8/$3.50 (in Canada)
V: THE PURSUIT OF DIANA
by Allen Wold
☐ 42401-9/$2.95   ☐ 43397-2/$3.50 (in Canada)
V: THE CHICAGO CONVERSION
by Geo. W. Proctor
☐ 42429-9/$2.95   ☐ 43417-0/$3.50 (in Canada)
V: THE FLORIDA PROJECT
by Tim Sullivan
☐ 42430-2/$2.95   ☐ 43418-9/$3.50 (in Canada)
V: PRISONERS AND PAWNS
by Howard Weinstein
☐ 42439-6/$2.95   ☐ 43420-0/$3.50 (in Canada)
V: THE ALIEN SWORDMASTER
by Somtow Sucharitkul
☐ 42441-8/$2.95   ☐ 43421-9/$3.50 (in Canada)
V: THE CRIVIT EXPERIMENT
by Alan Wold
☐ 42466-3/$2.95   ☐ 43441-3/$3.50 (in Canada)
V: THE NEW ENGLAND RESISTANCE
by Tim Sullivan
☐ 42467-1/$2.95   ☐ 43442-1/$3.50 (in Canada)
V: DEATH TIDE
by A.C. Crispin and D. Marshall
☐ 42469-8/$2.95   ☐ 43443-X/$3.50 (in Canada)
V: THE TEXAS RUN
by Geo W. Proctor
☐ 42470-1/$2.95   ☐ 43444-8/$3.50 (in Canada)

Buy them at your local bookstore or use this handy coupon
Clip and mail this page with your order

PINNACLE BOOKS, INC.
Post Office Box 690
Rockville Centre, NY 11571

Please send me the book(s) I have checked above. I am enclosing $_____(please add $1 to cover postage and handling). Send check or money order only—no cash or C.O.D.'s.

Mr./Mrs./Miss_____

Address_____

City_____State/Zip_____
Please allow six weeks for delivery. Prices subject to change without notice.